RAPTURE —
Get Right or Get Left

by
Dr. Hilton Sutton

Harrison House
Tulsa, Oklahoma

Unless otherwise indicated, all Scripture quotations are taken from the *King James Version* of the Bible.

6th Printing
Over 50,000 in Print

Rapture — Get Right or Get Left
ISBN 0-89274-877-X
(Formerly entitled *He's Coming* ISBN 0-89274-256-9)
Copyright 1983, 1991 © by Dr. Hilton Sutton
Hilton Sutton Ministries
736 Wilson Road
Humble, Texas 77338

Published by Harrison House, Inc.
P. O. Box 35035
Tulsa, Oklahoma 74153

Contents

PART I
The Seven Raptures

Introduction

I have yet to meet a person who does not believe in a rapture. Even those who say there will not be one, believe in it!

There are some fine men of God who teach that there is no rapture, saying the word *rapture* is not even in the Scriptures, which is true. But the Bible does talk about our being "caught up," or "gathered together unto the Lord," or Jesus "receiving us unto Himself." I am firmly convinced that there is more than enough evidence in the Scriptures to prove the reality of a rapture.

Every person who believes the Bible believes in the Rapture, whether he admits it or even realizes it. It is impossible to believe the Bible without believing in the Rapture because there are not one but seven raptures set forth in the Word.

However, there are leaders among us who teach that the Scripture is not to be interpreted literally.

Notice that the first three "catchings up" were indeed literal. Keep in mind that God is perfect in all that He does, and He says, **I change not** in Malachi 3:6. (See also Num. 23:19 and James 1:17.)

There are absolutely no Scriptures which indicate that the next Rapture (the rapture of the Church) will be any different than the three which preceded it. Those who teach other than what the Scriptures state are deceived.

Instead of the literal interpretation of Scriptures, some suggest that it can only be allegorically interpreted. The dictionary states that an *allegory* is "a symbolic story."

I ask the question, "Were Enoch, Elijah, and Jesus only symbolically caught up?" You know the answer. They were literally caught up!

Peter said there would come scoffers in the last days (see 2 Pet. 3:3) — and they have come! Some who would be our teachers have become scoffers, declaring there will be no Rapture, or at least not until the end of the Tribulation.

Deception reigns over the minds and spirits of those who oppose biblical truth.

We will look at each of the seven raptures as they are so vividly described in God's Word.

1

The First Rapture: Enoch

The first mention of a rapture in the Bible, found in the fifth chapter of the Book of Genesis, involves a man named Enoch. Let's examine what these Scriptures say about him.

> **And Enoch lived sixty and five years, and begat Methuselah: and Enoch walked with God after he begat Methuselah three hundred years, and begat sons and daughters:**
>
> **And all the days of Enoch were three hundred sixty and five years: and Enoch walked with God: and he was not;** *for God took him.*
>
> *Genesis 5:21-24*

These verses state, *God took him.* He walked with God for 365 years, and he did not die.

Let's look at the eleventh chapter of Hebrews. This chapter is often regarded as God's Hall of Fame of men and women of faith (and it is), but I do not believe it is complete. I am convinced that God's Hall of Fame of men and women of faith is still open and more are being added. (*Your* name may be up for consideration for inclusion in that hall, or it may be already written there!)

In Hebrews 11:5,6 we read:

> **By faith Enoch was translated that he should not see death; and was not found, because God had translated him: for before his translation he had this testimony, that he pleased God. But without faith it**

is impossible to please him (God): **for he that cometh to God must believe that he is, and that he is a rewarder of them that diligently seek him.**

By this we know that Enoch was taken *bodily* from the earth to heaven. He did not die, but was translated — received up unto the Lord physically alive. What would you call that, if not a rapture? There is no other way to interpret this verse, no way to explain it away without doing irreparable damage to the Scriptures. On the authority of both the Old and New Testaments, we can safely conclude: *Enoch walked with God: and he was not, for God raptured him.*

The Bible says Enoch was raptured because he walked with God all the years of his life and pleased Him. Enoch pleased God with his faith!

The Measure of Faith

If Enoch was raptured because he walked with and pleased God by faith, what is to keep believers today from having the same experience? Enoch was not born again or baptized with the Holy Spirit, yet God took him because of his faith.

There is no such thing as a born-again child of God who does not have faith. Romans 12:3 tells us, **God hath dealt to every man the measure of faith.** God gives *His* kind of faith — the *God-kind* of faith — the only kind He has.

We know the God-kind of faith is perfect and cannot be improved upon. There can't be anything wrong with *God's* kind of faith. And Romans 12:3 says God has given it to everyone.

You may ask, "How much is *the measure* of faith?" More than enough!

It is impossible for some to receive less than others. God deals to *every* man the measure of faith. Each receives the same amount.

Some people teach that certain ones receive more faith than others because "they need it." Not true. All of us receive the same amount of the God-kind of faith. When we first hear the Word of God, faith is activated. The first thing it produces for us is the born-again experience. We accept Jesus Christ and are saved by faith.

You may say, "But sometimes I feel like I don't have enough faith, and other times I feel like I don't have any faith at all." That is because you are depending upon your feelings instead of the Word of God. God says you have faith, so you do!

"Then there must be something wrong with my faith," you say. That is not the problem either. God has given you **the** *measure of faith;* that is more than enough. The problem lies with you: either you are not using the faith you have or you are using it improperly.

Let me give you an illustration. You buy a brand-new car. It is parked in your driveway, in perfect running order, full of gasoline, and ready to go. But instead of driving it, you walk. A car will do you no good unless you use it.

Sometimes we may not use our faith at all. At other times, we may use it improperly. (You can get into your car, but unless you operate it correctly, it will not work for you the way you want it to.) That does not mean we lack faith or that our faith is inferior. The problem lies in our application of the faith we already have.

Romans 10:17 says, **So then faith cometh by hearing, and hearing by the word of God.** The Word begins to work within us to activate our believing. Hearing and receiving the Word causes this God-given faith to become active within us. When faith is thus activated, it will produce; and its first product is salvation through the Holy Spirit. A person can be physically healed without faith — Scriptures bear that out — but he cannot be saved (born again) without it.

11

We can learn to use our faith properly by studying God's Word (which is our textbook), and by putting into action what we learn.

Enoch was able to please God *by faith*. Because of that, he was raptured to heaven — the first instance of a rapture in the Scriptures. Even those who claim there is no rapture taught in the Scriptures will agree with this one. We cannot build a doctrine on just this one passage of Scripture, but if we can find more than one reference to a rapture, we can. This was a true experience for Enoch. Let's look further to find out who else had a similar experience.

2

The Second Rapture: Elijah

The second rapture in the Bible was that of Elijah, the great prophet of God.

James describes Elijah as **a man subject to like passions as we are** (James 5:17). This means he was as human as you and I. As an example, let's look at an incident in 1 Kings 18.

Before his experience of being translated (caught up, snatched away, or raptured), Elijah was walking down a country road one day when the king's chariot pulled up. King Ahab leaned out, looked at Elijah, and said, "You're the man who is bringing all this trouble on Israel."

The prophet of God, a human being just like the rest of us, looked King Ahab in the eye and said boldly, "No, King, it is you! You have forsaken the Lord and have followed Baal. I want you and Jezebel — that ungodly, wicked woman you are living with — to gather up all the prophets of Baal and meet me tomorrow on Mount Carmel. We'll have a contest and see whose god is God!"

The Test

They all met on Mount Carmel. There were 450 prophets of Baal, tens of thousands of Israelites, and Elijah. Elijah had already decided he was the only one in all of Israel who had remained true to God.

There, on Mount Carmel, they prepared an altar. Elijah said, "You offer a sacrifice to your god; then I'll sacrifice to mine. The god who answers by fire and consumes the sacrifice is the god all of us will serve.''

The prophets of Baal prayed, chanted, and cried to their god until late afternoon. They worked themselves into such a frenzy that they actually cut themselves trying to get their god to act.

Elijah mocked them, ''You've had a good time today trying to get your god to do something, but perhaps he is away on a trip. Let me see what my God will do.''

He built a fresh altar, dug a trench around it, put wood on it, and placed a bullock on the wood. Then he had twelve barrels of water poured on the sacrifice until the trench around the altar was filled. When the time came to offer the sacrifice, Elijah stepped back and prayed a short prayer. Then fire from God fell from heaven, consumed the sacrifice, the wood, the stones, and licked up the water out of the ditch! The Israelites fell on their faces before God and repented. Then they took the prophets of Baal into the grove, and he slew them.

King Ahab jumped into his chariot and raced home at full speed. I can hear the brakes screech as he ground to a halt in front of the palace. He leaped out and bounded up the steps, where he met Queen Jezebel.

She took one look at Ahab's ashen white face and asked, ''What's the matter? What happened?'' Breathlessly, he told her the whole story. Ahab was white, but Jezebel turned fiery red! She sent a messenger to Elijah and said, ''As you have done to my prophets and priests, so will I do to you by this time tomorrow!'' (see 1 Kings 19:2.)

What do you suppose Elijah did at the threat of this evil, ungodly woman? Elijah — the great prophet of God for whom God had just done such mighty acts — took off running! Elijah was quite a runner, having once outrun the horses of Ahab's chariot. He ran until he dropped from exhaustion under the shade of a little tree.

As he lay there, he said, **O Lord, take away my life; for I am not better than my fathers** (1 Kings 19:4). In other words, "Go ahead and kill me, God. If You don't, Jezebel will!"

After he slept for a while, an angel woke him with a hot plate lunch from heaven's cafeteria. Then Elijah went on his way, refreshed.

Jezebel did not succeed in her threats. God saw to it that Elijah was victorious. Jezebel and Ahab were destroyed, just as Elijah had foretold.

There is a lesson in this for us today: never let the threats of the devil determine your lifestyle, set your mental attitude, or affect your relationship with God. The devil is a deceiver. He loves to lie and he usually does it with threats. If you allow him to get by with it, he will use threats to destroy you and your effectiveness for God.

As time passed, God spoke to Elijah about a young man named Elisha, who was to succeed him as prophet of Israel. They worked together until the time came for Elijah to pass his prophet's mantle on to Elisha. We read about this in 2 Kings 2:1,8-11:

> **And it came to pass, when the Lord would take up Elijah into heaven by a whirlwind, that Elijah went with Elisha from Gilgal. And Elijah took his mantle, and wrapped it together, and smote the waters, and they were divided hither and thither, so that they two went over on dry ground.**
>
> **And it came to pass, when they were gone over, that Elijah said unto Elisha, Ask what I shall do for thee, before *I be taken away from thee.* And Elisha said, I pray thee, let a double portion of thy spirit be upon me.**
>
> **And he said, Thou hast asked a hard thing: nevertheless, if thou see me *when I am taken from thee,* it shall be so unto thee; but if not, it shall not be so.**

And it came to pass, as they still went on, and talked, that, behold, there appeared a chariot of fire, and horses of fire, and parted them both asunder; and Elijah went up by a whirlwind into heaven.

Anyone who believes the Bible will have to accept that God translated both Enoch and Elijah, bodily and alive, from earth to heaven. In other words, they were raptured. This is the second of the seven biblical raptures.

3

The Third Rapture: Jesus

The record of the third rapture is found in Acts, chapter 1. On the Sabbath, Jesus and His disciples left the city of Jerusalem and went out to the Mount of Olives. Paul tells us there was a company of more than five hundred who went out with Him (see 1 Cor. 15:6). There Jesus conveyed His last great message to them. (Read the final chapters of Matthew, Mark, Luke, and chapter 1 of Acts.)

And when he had spoken these things, while they beheld, he was taken up; and a cloud received him out of their sight.

And while they looked steadfastly toward heaven as he went up, behold, two men stood by them in white apparel; which also said, Ye men of Galilee, why stand ye gazing up into heaven? this same Jesus which is taken up from you into heaven, shall so come in like manner as ye have seen him go into heaven.

Acts 1:9-11

Again, this is a passage of Scripture that no one, even those who do not believe in the Rapture, can discount.

Jesus was taken up alive, bodily. He had been resurrected for forty days. During that time, He had walked on earth, been with His disciples on several occasions, cooked for them, and even eaten with them the same foods He had eaten before His crucifixion.

He seemed to be very natural, yet He had supernatural abilities — He was in his earthly glorified body! When He

17

appeared to His disciples in a closed room, He did not open the door, but passed through the wall (see John 20:25-28). He had the unique ability to appear and disappear at will. Mark 16:19; Luke 24:50,51; along with Acts 1:9-11 clearly establish that Jesus was caught up alive from earth to heaven — in His glorified body.

He was in His glorified body at the time of His ascension. However, nothing in the Scriptures indicates that Enoch and Elijah were in glorified bodies when they were taken up. Since Jesus is our example, the Church at its rapture will be in a glorified state, as was Jesus (see 1 Cor. 15:50-53; 1 John 3:1-3).

Ephesians 5:27 says the Lord will present unto Himself **a glorious church, not having spot, or wrinkle, or any such thing; but that it should be holy and without blemish.** I do not teach that we will be glorified before the Rapture and have glorified bodies. We will, however, be like Him *when we see Him* (see 1 John 3:2). The instant Jesus appears with a shout, we, by the energies of the Holy Spirit, will overcome the natural law of gravity and, in that same instant, will become glorified, departing earth for heaven.

Three biblical accounts of raptures should be enough evidence to establish for anyone the reality of raptures. If God has already raptured three of His saints, including His own Son, why should we not believe He will also rapture us? We are clearly told in the Scriptures that He is going to catch away the Church. Our rapture — the rapture of the Church — is Rapture Number Four. But first let's look at Rapture Number Five.

4

The Fifth Rapture: The Great Multitude

The fifth rapture is the gathering together unto the Lord, or the catching up from earth to heaven, of the mid-Tribulation saints. It is recorded in Revelation 7, verses 9-17:

> After this I beheld, and, lo, a great multitude, which no man could number, of all nations, and kindreds, and people, and tongues, stood before the throne, and before the Lamb, clothed with white robes, and palms in their hands; and cried with a loud voice, saying, Salvation to our God which sitteth upon the throne, and unto the Lamb.

> And all the angels stood round about the throne, and about the elders and the four beasts, and fell before the throne on their faces, and worshipped God, saying, Amen: Blessing, and glory, and wisdom, and thanksgiving, and honour, and power, and might, be unto our God for ever and ever, Amen.

> And one of the elders answered saying unto me, What are these which are arrayed in white robes? and whence came they?

> And I said unto him, Sir, thou knowest. And he said to me, These are they which came out of great tribulation, and have washed their robes, and made them white in the blood of the Lamb.

> Therefore are they before the throne of God, and serve him day and night in his temple: and he that sitteth on the throne shall dwell among them.

> **They shall hunger no more, neither thirst any
> more; neither shall the sun light on them, nor any heat.
> For the Lamb which is in the midst of the throne shall
> feed them, and shall lead them unto living fountains
> of waters: and God shall wipe away all tears from their
> eyes.**

From this reference, we learn a fact that many do not
know: a great number of people, probably about one billion,
will be saved during the first three and one-half years of
the Tribulation Period (a time I call "God's Master
Performance"). Nowhere in the Scriptures is this exact
figure given; it is a purely hypothetical estimate arrived at
by computation based on the following end-time prophecy
of Zechariah:

> **Thus saith the Lord of hosts; In those days** (the
> Tribulation Period) **it shall come to pass, that *ten men
> shall take hold* out of all languages of the nations, even
> shall take hold of the skirt *of him that is a Jew,* saying,
> We will go with you: for we have heard that God is
> with you.**
>
> **Zechariah 8:23**

If there are 25 million Jews on earth during the
Tribulation and ten Gentile men (plus women and children)
are saved for every Jew, the total number saved would be
approximately one billion. The Bible says it will be a **great
multitude, which no man could number, of all nations, and
kindreds, and people, and tongues.** These are the ones who
will stand before the throne of God, **clothed with white
robes, and palms in their hands.**

This company (as tradition would have it) is not the
Church of Jesus Christ. Rapture Number Four will take place
before the Tribulation. This multitude will be saved during
the first half of the Tribulation through the ministry of the
144,000 unmarried Jewish evangelists (see Rev. 7 and 14).

Mid-Tribulation Saints

There is no question but that a great multitude is caught up at the midpoint of the Tribulation. When the Antichrist breaks his agreement with the nation of Israel, becoming hostile to them, and moves to destroy the mid-Tribulation saints, God intervenes by snatching them away to heaven. (It is very difficult to make war against someone who is no longer around!) God frustrates the devil's plan by simply taking these saints out of the way.

When we carefully look at the description of those who are involved in this fifth rapture, we see clearly that they are not the redeemed Church of Jesus Christ. These people do not fit any of the descriptions of the Body of Christ given in 1 Thessalonians 4 or Revelation 4 and 5.

Jesus does not meet them in the air, as He does His Church. There is no sounding of the trumpet at their rapture, nor is there an accompanying resurrection. They are not presented with crowns of gold; they do not sit on thrones; they do not sing the new song (they sing the song of Moses and the Lamb). It is strictly said of them: **These are they which** *came out of great tribulation,* **and have washed their robes, and made them white in the blood of the Lamb** (Rev. 7:14).

This verse suggests that these people already had robes of righteousness which they had soiled. (Otherwise, why would they need to cleanse them?) This is not the Church company. These are the Tribulation saints — Israelis and prodigals — the multitudes who had been brought into some encounter with the things of God and who had been unfaithful servants. All such "foolish virgins" who had not been looking for the return of our Lord can be put into this category (see Matt. 25:1-10). Their robes, which were soiled, had to be cleansed in the blood of the Lamb.

But this is not a description of the saints of the Church of Jesus Christ. The saints of the Church Age are clearly described in Ephesians 5:27 and Revelation 4 and 5. They have crowns of gold; they sit upon thrones; they wear white robes; and they sing the new song, confessing to Jesus.

> **Thou art worthy ... for thou wast slain, and hast redeemed us to God by thy blood out of every kindred, and tongue, and people, and nation; and hast made us unto our God kings and priests: and we shall reign on the earth.**
>
> **Revelation 5:9,10**

Many of these mid-Tribulation saints have already been redeemed; they were earthlings. There is quite a difference between the Church and this great mid-Tribulation company which is taken up to escape the wrath of the devil through the Antichrist. This should be crystal clear. The rapture of these Tribulation saints is Rapture Number Five.

5

The Sixth Rapture:
The 144,000

Rapture Number Six is the rapture of the 144,000 Jewish evangelists, who are described in Revelation, chapters 7 and 14:

> And after these things I saw four angels standing on the four corners of the earth, holding the four winds of the earth, that the wind should not blow in the earth, nor on the sea, nor on any tree.
>
> And I saw another angel ascending from the east, having the seal of the living God: and he cried with a loud voice to the four angels, to whom it was given to hurt the earth and the sea, saying, Hurt not the earth, neither the sea, nor the trees, till we have sealed the servants of our God in their foreheads.
>
> And I heard the number of them which were sealed: and there were sealed *an hundred and forty and four thousand* of all the tribes of the children of Israel.
>
> Revelation 7:1-4
>
> And I looked, and, lo a Lamb stood on the mount Sion, and with him *an hundred forty and four thousand*, having his Father's name written in their foreheads.
>
> And I heard a voice from heaven, as the voice of many waters, and as the voice of a great thunder: and I heard the voice of harpers harping with their harps: and they sung as it were a new song before the throne, and before the four beasts, and the elders: and no man could learn that song but *the hundred and forty and four thousand*, which were redeemed from the earth.

These are they which were not defiled with women; for they are virgins. These are they which follow the Lamb whithersoever he goeth. These were redeemed from among men, being the firstfruits unto God and to the Lamb.

And in their mouth was found no guile: for they are without fault before the throne of God.
[Note that verse 5 places the 144,000 before the throne of God — no longer on the earth.]

Revelation 14:1-5

These passages clearly describe the rapture of the 144,000 Jewish evangelists when they have finished their ministry. The primary ministry of these 144,000 was to the people of Israel. During the seven-year period we call the Tribulation (God's Master Performance), God ministers directly to Israel through these 144,000 chosen Jewish evangelists.

Ministry to Israel

During these seven years, God deals with the Jewish nation of Israel; but Gentiles may come in also if they so choose. As it is now, the ministry of God is through the Church. But once the Church is taken up, God will return to complete His ministry with Israel. He will have only seven years in which to complete it.[1] During that time, if Gentiles want to be saved, they will have to come in through the method God will use to bring all of Israel back to Himself.

This is how simple it is. Today Jews are not excluded from coming into the Church. But when God has finished His direct work with the Gentiles, He will have to complete the last seven years of His determined work on behalf of Israel. All of this is described in Daniel 9:24-27. An important key to understanding Daniel's prophetic time frame is to know that Daniel's days are years. His 70 weeks are weeks of years, not days. Were they days, there would not be sufficient time for the events of his prophecy to come to

24

pass. Convert his days to years, and one has a right amount of time for his events to come to pass.

God must finish His work in behalf of Israel. However, as the Prophet Zechariah revealed, during the first half of this seven-year period, ten times as many Gentile men (not counting women and children) as Jews will come into the Kingdom. These converts make up the great multitude (the fifth rapture) who stand before God's throne, as described in Revelation chapter 7.

When the 144,000 have finished their ministry both to Israel and many Gentiles, Jesus joins them at Mount Zion (See Rev. 14:1). They learn the new song which the Church has been singing. This is the only group, besides the Church of Jesus Christ, permitted to learn the new song (see Rev. 14:3).

This tells us the approximate time they reach heaven. They arrive in time to learn the new song and join the Church at the wedding ceremony of the Lamb, which occurs near the beginning of the fifth year of the seven-year Tribulation Period (see Rev. 19). The ministry of the 144,000 lasts for approximately four of those seven years. (We will deal with these events in more detail later in this book.)

With the taking up of the 144,000, we have Rapture Number Six. There is a difference in the raptures we have discussed. The first three involved individuals —Enoch, Elijah, and Jesus. Raptures Five and Six involved great multitudes of people. It is just as easy for God to take up a great multitude as to rapture an individual. Quantity is no problem to God.

---

[1]A study of Daniel 9:24-27 reveals God's period of 490 years (70 weeks, with each lasting 7 years), in which He is determined to accomplish the six things listed in verse 24. There are fixed events in this passage, clearly establishing a remainder of 7 years.

6

The Seventh Rapture:
The Two Witnesses

Rapture Number Seven is the rapture of the two witnesses, found in Revelation 11:3-12:

> And I will give power unto *my two witnesses*, and they shall prophesy a thousand two hundred and threescore days, clothed in sackcloth.

> These are the two olive trees, and the two candlesticks standing before the God of the earth.

> And if any man will hurt them, fire proceedeth out of their mouth, and devoureth their enemies: and if any man will hurt them, he must in this manner be killed.

> These have power to shut heaven, that it rain not in the days of their prophecy: and have power over waters to turn them to blood, and to smite the earth with all plagues, as often as they will.

> And when they shall have finished their testimony, the beast that ascendeth out of the bottomless pit shall make war against them, and shall overcome them, and kill them. And their dead bodies shall lie in the street of the great city, which spiritually is called Sodom and Egypt, where also our Lord was crucified.

> And they of the people and kindreds and tongues and nations shall see their dead bodies three days and an half, and shall not suffer their dead bodies to be put in graves.

> And they that dwell upon the earth shall rejoice over them, and make merry, and shall send gifts one to another; because these two prophets tormented them that dwelt on the earth.
>
> And after three days and an half the Spirit of life from God entered into them, and they stood upon their feet; and great fear fell upon them which saw them. And they heard a great voice from heaven saying unto them, Come up hither.
>
> And they *ascended up to heaven in a cloud;* and their enemies beheld them.

Once the Antichrist has broken his agreement with Israel, he invades the nation and sets up headquarters in a temple at Jerusalem. Immediately, two men appear in the street before the Temple and begin a countdown of judgment against the Antichrist. Unsuccessfully, the Antichrist tries to destroy them. Only four days before the end of that seven-year period, he again sends his security forces against these two men. This time God allows them to be killed.

The World Watches

For three and one-half days, their dead bodies lie in the street, while the crowds who follow the Antichrist celebrate by exchanging gifts and making merry, saying, "Those two who tormented us are dead and we are glad!" The entire world views the scene as it is undoubtedly broadcast on television via satellite.

After those three and one-half days, with the television cameras still operating, life from God reenters those dead bodies and they are resurrected, while the whole world watches! The two witnesses stand alive as God's voice is heard from heaven: "Come up here!" Then the two witnesses ascend, just as those before them — Enoch, Elijah, Jesus, the Church, the 144,000 Jewish evangelists, and the Tribulation saints.

Imagine how shocked those TV cameramen will be as they start panning the ascension, following the two witnesses up, up, all the way to heaven! As the skies roll back like a scroll, the world looks right into the face of God! (See. Rev. 6:12-17.)

Then there occurs an upheaval of nature like the world has never known. Jesus comes charging back to earth, with all His angels and the saints who have been there with Him. Back to earth they come! What an event to behold!

We have six raptures on record — enough to convince any jury. But God's number is not six; it is seven. Look now at Rapture Number Four, which will give us a total of seven.

7

The Fourth Rapture:
The Church

People who say the Church will not be raptured are in an unpleasant position. They believe the Church will experience the seven years of Tribulation and then, on that final day, at the seventh and last angelic trumpet, be taken to meet Christ in the air, only to come right back down with Him.

Such a belief does not seem reasonable to me. If there is no Rapture, we will never get to heaven. If we never get to heaven, a major portion of John's Revelation should be torn out and thrown away, because chapters four and five reveal events in heaven in which the Church must participate. In fact, there is no further reference to the Church until Revelation 19. The Wedding of the Lamb and the Marriage Supper are two events that take place in heaven, not on earth (see Rev. 19). If the Church is to take part in these glorious events, it must be raptured *before* the Tribulation.

Someone has asked, "But doesn't Paul teach that we will be caught up *in a moment, in the twinkling of an eye, at the last trump* (1 Cor. 15:52)? Yes, he does.

"Well, wouldn't that be the seventh angelic trumpet mentioned in Revelation 11?" No, it would not.

The seventh angelic trumpet of Revelation 11 does not sound until the final day of the Tribulation — the day Jesus comes back to earth. If there were seven years before the

31

Church is taken to heaven, we would not be there to participate in any of the heavenly events revealed in Revelation. What, then, would we do with all those heavenly events?

This is one of the great problems in the Church today. Many will not accept any reality in the Bible. To them, everything is interpreted figuratively! The devil is doing his best right now to strip away all reality from the Church and disguise everything in God's Word under a cloak of symbolism.

A Literal Event

Some things in Revelation are described in symbolic language, but certain events described in the Word are not to be taken figuratively or allegorically. They are foretold in literal terms and are meant to be taken literally. The catching away of the Church is a literal event.

The appearing of Jesus Christ in the heavens is a literal event. In John 14:3, Jesus told His disciples, **And if I go and prepare a place for you,** *I will come again,* **and receive you unto myself;** *that where I am, there ye may be also.* Had He never gone away, we would have little reason to believe the rest of His statement. But He did go away as He said He would, and we have every reason to believe He will come again. One half of His prophecy was accurately fulfilled. Why doubt that the other half will be fulfilled?

Jesus said He would come again to receive us unto Himself. When He said that, He was speaking to His followers. *We* are His followers. He is coming back for *us!*

He said, **I will come again, and receive you unto myself; that where I am** (please note the terminology), **there ye may be also.** This clearly indicates a change of position for us. Jesus' appearing is literal; likewise, our being in heaven with Him is literal.

In 1 Corinthians 15:51-53, Paul wrote these words concerning the Rapture of the Church:

> **Behold, I shew you a mystery; We shall not all sleep (die), but we shall all be changed, In a moment, in the twinkling of an eye, *at the last trump: for the trumpet shall sound*, and the dead shall be raised incorruptible, and we shall be changed.**
>
> **For this corruptible must put on incorruption, and this mortal must put on immortality.**

He also touched on this subject while writing to the Thessalonians:

> **For this we say unto you by the word of the Lord, that we which are alive and remain unto the *coming of the Lord* shall not prevent (precede) them which are asleep.**
>
> **For the Lord himself shall descend from heaven with a shout, with the voice of the archangel, and *with the trump of God*: and the dead in Christ shall rise first:**
>
> **Then we which are alive and remain shall be caught up together with them in the clouds, to meet the Lord in the air: and so shall we ever be with the Lord.**
>
> **1 Thessalonians 4:15-17**

The Last Trumpet

Both times Paul refers to the last trumpet, or the trump of God. These are one and the same because the event is the same — the appearing of our Lord for His Church.

Study carefully the seventh angelic trumpet of Revelation 11 and you will make a discovery: the events surrounding the seventh trumpet are *not* the same as those surrounding the last trumpet of God. The last trumpet is God's final signal to welcome the Church into heaven.

If we were not going to be taken up until the sounding of the final angelic trumpet on the last day of the Tribulation Period, we would never get to heaven and participate in the heavenly events. We would not attend the Wedding of the Lamb and the Marriage Supper, or sing the new song, or witness the opening of the seals.

Jesus said of His appearing, **Of that day and hour knoweth no man, no, not the angels of heaven, but my Father only** (Matt. 24:36). Were we not caught up until the sounding of the seventh angelic trumpet on the final day of this seven-year period, anyone who had studied the Book of Revelation and chapter 14 of Zechariah would be able to calculate the very day and hour that Jesus would return and stand on the Mount of Olives.

All of this is spelled out in the Scriptures. The final day of the seven-year period has a perfect chronological order from early morning to evening. Those seven years are a fixed period of time, exactly seven years — or 84 months, or 2,520 days — divided into two halves of 3 1/2 years — or 42 months, or 1,260 days each.

Even if one were on earth during that period and did not get his countdown started at the beginning, he would have no problem calculating from midpoint. There will be two witnesses in Jerusalem who are counting down the days to Christ's return and His destruction of the Antichrist (see Rev. 11:1-13). One could pick up on their countdown and know exactly what day Jesus would return to earth.

Jesus said no one will know the day and hour of His *appearing*, but His *return* is clearly laid out in the Scriptures. The prophetic Scriptures (Zech. 14 and Rev. 19 and 20) tell of Christ's *return*, not His *appearing* to receive His Church! These are two separate and distinct events.

There is a major distinction between the "last trump," which is the "trumpet of God" heralding the Rapture of the Church, and the seventh angelic trumpet which precedes Christ's return to earth in judgment.

Since the Church will have already been raptured to heaven — the fourth rapture — it (the Church) will be prepared to return in triumph with Christ at His Second Coming, as stated in Zechariah 14:5 and Revelation 17:14 and 19:14.[1]

---

[1]The Church is the army of Revelation 19:14, based on a number of Scriptures (Song of Sol. 6:4; 2 Cor. 10:4; Eph. 6:10-18; 2 Tim. 2:1-4; Rev. 2:26,27).

8

Understanding
What the Bible Teaches
About the Rapture
of the Church

To determine where the Rapture of the Church occurs in relation to the seven-year Tribulation Period, we need to look at Daniel 9:24-27. (See also 2 Thess. 2:1-9 and Rev. 4-6.) As we study these Scriptures, we will understand that this seven-year period cannot even begin as long as the Church is still on earth.

Daniel's Prophecy
of the End Time

Seventy weeks are determined upon thy people and upon thy holy city, to finish the transgression, and to make an end of sins, and to make reconciliation for iniquity, and to bring in everlasting righteousness, and to seal up the vision and prophecy, and to anoint the most Holy.

Know therefore and understand, that from the going forth of the commandment to restore and to build Jerusalem unto the Messiah the Prince shall be seven weeks, and threescore and two weeks: the street shall be built again, and the wall, even in troublous times.

And after threescore and two weeks shall Messiah be cut off, but not for himself: and the people of the prince that shall come shall destroy the city and the sanctuary; and the end thereof shall be with a flood, and unto the end of the war desolations are determined.

And he shall confirm the covenant with many for one week: and in the midst of the week he shall cause the sacrifice and the oblation to cease, and for the overspreading of abominations he shall make it desolate, even until the consummation, and that determined shall be poured upon the desolate.

Daniel 9:24-27

God is revealing His determined dealings with Israel. He reveals to Daniel that it covers a period of 70 weeks, with (each day a year) each week lasting 7 years, making a total of 490 years. God also reveals to Daniel exactly when that period will begin. He uses a fixed event which even secular history records: the Persian king allowing Jewish slaves, led by Zerubbabel, Ezra and Nehemiah to rebuild the city of Jerusalem. That is the signal event which begins the 490-year period.

Then God reveals to Daniel that 483 of those years (or 69 full weeks) will be ended when the Messiah, the great Prince, is "cut off" in Jerusalem (the Crucifixion). That leaves just one week, exactly seven years of the original period, to be fulfilled.

What Happened to the Final Week? Why Has it Not Yet Been Fulfilled?

With the Crucifixion, God ushered in the Age of the Church. Between the years 483 and 484 of that 490-year span, God brought in the Church Age. Between the end of week 69 and the beginning of week 70 comes the era of the Church. God has left Himself only one week (seven years) after the Church Age in which to finish His direct dealings with Israel. It is during this time that all six major events of Daniel 9:24 must be fulfilled.

God originally gave Himself 490 years to accomplish these six events, yet 483 of those years have passed and He still has not accomplished them. That leaves only seven years for Him to fulfill the six prophecies on behalf of Israel. There is no doubt that He will do it. In fact, He has already begun the prelude to this fulfillment.

In Daniel 9:26,27, another prince comes on the scene and enters into agreement with Israel. This prince is of Satan. Satan can do nothing without a human being as his instrument — thus enters the Antichrist, Satan's choice agent. According to Paul's letter to the Thessalonians, this "man of sin" cannot be revealed to cause "the overspreading of abominations" until the Church has first been removed from the earth. Daniel places the beginning of Antichrist's activity at the onset of the last seven years of God's work with Israel.

Paul's Description of the Rapture

In 2 Thessalonians 2, Paul's writing cleared up some misconceptions that had arisen concerning the return of Christ to reign on earth. The Thessalonians were in a state of theological confusion. Paul had gone there and taught them correctly, but in his absence, someone else had come in, saying that Christ had already returned and that the day of Christ was "at hand."

Upon learning of their confusion and anxiety, Paul wrote a letter to set their thinking straight concerning the end times and the Lord's return. He speaks of the day of Christ and outlines the events which must precede that day:

> **Now we beseech you, brethren, by the coming of our Lord Jesus Christ, and by our gathering together unto him, That ye be not soon shaken in mind, or be troubled, neither by spirit, nor by word, nor by letter as from us, as that the day of Christ is at hand.**

> **Let no man deceive you by any means: for that day**
> **shall not come, except there come a falling away first,**
> **and that man of sin be revealed, the son of perdition;**
> **Who opposeth and exalteth himself above all that is**
> **called God, or that is worshipped; so that he as God**
> **sitteth in the temple of God, shewing himself that he**
> **is God.**
>
> **2 Thessalonians 2:1-4**

In verse 1, Paul talks about the day of Christ's appearing, at which time the Church is gathered together unto Him. Then he goes on to say, "But you have become confused by those who have been teaching you that the day of Christ is at hand, that He has already returned and is here right now."

Some teachers today teach that all Scriptures on the Second Coming are fulfilled when a person accepts Christ into his heart. They teach a figurative return of Christ, who comes back to earth spiritually by entering the hearts of believers.

Teaching such as this is one reason why you and I need to study the Word of God for ourselves! Nowhere in the Bible is there any indication that receiving Christ into your heart fulfills the Scriptures concerning either the appearing of Jesus or the Second Coming.

Some believe it is a spiritual thing. But we have seen in Acts 1:11 that when Jesus ascended bodily into heaven, there were angels standing among the Galileans who said to them, **This same Jesus, which is taken up from you into heaven,** *shall so come in like manner as ye have seen him go into heaven.* That is not a spiritual thing; it is a reality — a spiritual reality.

The devil is trying to steal away reality and, at the same time, steal away the authority of the Scriptures.

Paul said to the Church in Thessalonica, "Someone has taught you mistakenly. He may have been a sincere man of God, but he has not taught you properly. I taught you correctly, that the day of Christ cannot come until first there be a 'falling away' and the 'man of sin' be revealed" (see 2 Thess. 2). If we stop at verse 4 of this chapter, it appears that Paul is saying Christ cannot come at all until there has been a "falling away" and the "man of sin" has been revealed. If that is so, the Church will still be here during the Tribulation under the Antichrist! But I have never been under the Antichrist and I never will be. I am under God!

Let's read on:

> **Remember ye not, that, when I was yet with you, I told you these things?**
>
> **And now ye know what withholdeth that he** (the Antichrist) **might be revealed in his time.**
>
> **For the mystery of iniquity doth already work: only he who now letteth will let, until he be taken out of the way.**
>
> **And then shall that Wicked be revealed, whom the Lord shall consume with the spirit of his mouth, and shall destroy with the brightness of his coming: even him, whose coming is after the working of Satan with all power and signs and lying wonders.**
>
> **2 Thessalonians 2:5-9**

Paul states that this "man of sin," whom the Lord will destroy with the brightness of His coming, cannot be revealed to begin his activity, until that which has been withholding him has been taken out of the way.[1] Something is restraining the Antichrist to keep him from coming forth prematurely. When that withholder, or restrainer, has been taken out of the way (and not one day sooner), then the "man of sin" will be revealed. He will be free to go about his evil activities until Christ comes to destroy him with the brightness of His coming.

The Church Restraining the Antichrist

And now ye know what withholdeth that he might be revealed in his time. For the mystery of iniquity doth already work: only he who now letteth will let, until he be taken out of the way. And then shall that Wicked (one) be revealed.

2 Thessalonians 2:6,7

Most of those who teach against the Rapture of the Church say this "restrainer" or "withholder," which is to be taken out of the way, is the Holy Spirit. But that is impossible for several reasons.

The Holy Ghost is God.[2] The unique character of God the Holy Ghost — the Third Person of the Trinity — allows Him to be present everywhere at all times. He cannot be "taken out" or "put in." The psalmist says of God:

Whither shall I go from thy spirit? or whither shall I flee from thy presence? If I ascend up into heaven, thou art there: if I make my bed in hell, behold, thou art there.

Psalm 139:7,8

The Holy Spirit cannot be removed from the earth — certainly not while the Church is still here!

If the Holy Ghost were to be taken so the Antichrist could be revealed to carry out his seven-year satanic plan, then nobody could be saved during that time, because the Scripture says that no one can be saved unless he is drawn by God (see John 6:44). How could God draw people to salvation if His Spirit had already departed? If God's Spirit had been removed from the earth, how could all of these people be saved? They could not!

The Church — that company of born-again, Spirit-filled, Spirit-led followers of Jesus through whom God is working to reach the masses of people today — will be taken out of the way. The anointed Church is the restrainer, withholding unrestrained lawlessness in this hour.

Paul said, **The mystery of iniquity doth already work** (2 Thess. 2:7). The spirit of lawlessness, which is Satan's desire to bring forth the Antichrist, is already present. *The only thing withholding an eruption of lawlessness in the earth today, such as we have never seen, is the presence of the Church of Jesus Christ!*

The Church, right now, is getting stronger and stronger. Not only are we increasing in number, but we are learning more and more about the authority of God's Word and how to exercise that godly authority.

Paul told Timothy to pray **for all that are in authority; that we may lead a quiet and peaceable life in all godliness and honesty** (1 Tim. 2:2). In the last few years, the Church has begun to put that authority into force.

If you will start doing what the Word of God tells you to do, you will begin to see God advance and the works of the devil diminish!

The Church is the withholder, and it has successfully withheld the devil's best plan for more than 1,900 years. What a track record!

From Joel, chapter 2:28-31, we learn that once the Holy Spirit begins His earthly work through believers, the outpouring continues up to the final day of the Tribulation — the day when the sun becomes black and the moon becomes as blood (see Rev. 6:12-17). This is absolute proof that the Holy Spirit is not removed from the earth before the Tribulation. Therefore, the only other choice for removal is the anointed Church.

The Church in Heaven

In Revelation, chapters 4 and 5, the Apostle John describes the Church in heaven. They are represented by the 24 elders.[3]

The full description of these 24 elders fits every believer. They have to be representatives because the number 24 is, itself, a symbolic figure. But even without the number 24 being symbolic of the Church, the word *elder*, alone, is enough to indicate that this passage does not refer literally to 24 men. In the New Testament, an elder always represents the Church before God. The 24 elders are not a company complete within themselves; they are just representatives of the Church which is in heaven.

The Church itself is mentioned in chapters 4 and 5 of Revelation. Chapter 4, verse 6, refers to **a sea of glass like unto crystal.** As a result of an intensive study of the Scriptures, I see this crystal sea as a symbol of the Church before the throne of God. The verses before and after this passage make it evident that the word *sea* does not refer to a literal body of water, but rather symbolizes a mass of people. In fact, this is true throughout the Scriptures. Whenever the word *sea* is used in the Bible, unless it identifies a known body of water which can be located geographically, it always refers to a mass of people. In this particular case, it is called a **crystal** sea.

It is appropriate that John should symbolize the Church as a crystal sea, because crystal is the only earthly substance in which a flaw cannot go undetected. Flaws in other substances — diamonds, rubies, sapphires, emeralds, platinum, gold, silver, fine brass — may be hidden, but not in crystal. The nature of crystal is such that it magnifies a flaw. As a collector of crystal, particularly antique cut glass, I can verify this. John chose well his symbol of the Church. Paul wrote in Ephesians 5:27 that when Jesus presents the Church to Himself, it will be a **glorious church, not having spot, or wrinkle, or any such thing; but that it should be holy and** *without blemish.*

So we see the Church in heaven just as Paul said it would have to be before the Antichrist could begin his activity. Daniel said the Antichrist would start work at the beginning of the seven-year period. In Thessalonians, we see that the Antichrist cannot begin his activity until the withholding factor is taken out of the way. By properly analyzing these Scriptures, with the help of the Holy Spirit, we see that "the withholder" is the Church of Jesus Christ.

In Revelation, chapters 4 and 5, we find a description of the great scene before the throne of God. The Church is there *with all of the angels.* This is significant because in Hebrews 1:14 we learn that angels are **ministering spirits, sent forth to minister for them who shall be heirs of salvation** — in other words, *us!*

Angels are on direct assignment from God to minister for those who shall be called heirs of salvation. The angels have proven their loyalty to God; they will not fail on their assignment.

Since John sees *all* of the angels in heaven before the throne of God, the Church would have to be there also. Otherwise, the Church would be left on earth without the "ministering spirits." If the Church were still here, then the angels would still be here too, right where they are at this moment, taking care of their ministry assignment on our behalf.

John tells us in Revelation 5:11, **the number of them** (the angels) **was ten thousand times ten thousand, and thousands of thousands.** If 100 billion angels are in heaven, all at the same time, that means everybody they had been assigned to protect or to minister to would be there also.

The Antichrist Released

And I saw when the Lamb opened one of the seals, and I heard, as it were the noise of thunder, one of the four beasts saying, Come and see.

> And I saw, and behold a white horse: and he that
> sat on him had a bow; and a crown was given unto
> him: and he went forth conquering, and to conquer.
>
> Revelation 6:1,2

Here Jesus opens the first seal of the book He has taken
from His Father's hand. When He opens the seal, the man
destined to be the Antichrist is released. According to Daniel
9:24-27, this occurs at the beginning of this seven-year
period known as the Great Tribulation. That tells us the
exact time Jesus will be opening the first seal.

Several things must take place before the Antichrist can
begin his activity. The Church has to be taken up to heaven
to stand in front of the throne of God, observing as Jesus
opens the first seal. When it is opened, the Antichrist is
released. If Jesus never opened that first seal, the Antichrist
could never start, whether we were up there or not. But
Jesus will not open the seal until we are there.

To confirm what I have just described, let's look at
Hebrews 12:22-24:

> But ye are come unto mount Sion, and unto the
> city of the living God, the heavenly Jerusalem, and to
> an innumerable company of angels.
>
> To the general assembly and church of the
> firstborn, which are written in heaven, and to God the
> Judge of all, and to the spirits of just men made perfect,
>
> And to Jesus the mediator of the new covenant,
> and to the blood of sprinkling, that speaketh better
> things than that of Abel.

We see Paul describing the same scene in heaven that John
has described in chapters 4 and 5 of Revelation. In three
verses, Paul gives a description that takes John two full
chapters to relate. But it confirms that, at the same time,
all the angels are in heaven with *the general assembly and
church of the firstborn*. Praise God!

Summary

These are the seven raptures:

1. Enoch
2. Elijah
3. Jesus
4. The Church of Jesus Christ (the middle rapture, the one to which we refer when we speak of the Rapture)
5. The mid-Tribulation saints
6. The 144,000 Jewish evangelists
7. The two witnesses (on the final day of the Tribulation Period)

In Part II of this book, we will contrast Jesus' appearing in the heavens to rapture His Church (before the Great Tribulation) with His return to earth to establish His kingdom.

---

[1]Verse 3 tells us plainly that the Antichrist must be revealed. Verse 6 declares that he is to be revealed *in his time*. His time is the fixed period of seven years, not part of the Church Age.

[2]The Holy Spirit, or God the Holy Ghost, is just as much God as God the Father or God the Son.

[3]Why 24 elders representing the Church? Twelve to represent the righteous of the tribes of Israel and 12 to represent the New Testament saints. The New Jerusalem described in Revelation 21 includes both companies (see vv. 12,14).

Part II
The Second Coming
of Jesus

Introduction

No other subject in the Word of God is more exciting and important to a child of God than the appearing in glory of our Savior and Lord (see Titus 2:13).

We are, of course, excited about the wonderful salvation that is ours through the Lord Jesus Christ and about the marvelous infilling of the Holy Spirit that so many believers across the nation are enjoying. But it is equally exciting to know that Jesus Christ, the Son of God, is going to appear in the heavens and that the true Church will be caught up from the earth with the angels. Then we will be escorted to meet Him in the air and proceed with Him to the throne of God.

It is also exciting to know that Jesus Christ will return to establish His government here on earth. The prophecies of Isaiah 9:6 will be fulfilled: **The government shall be upon His shoulder.** But before He can take the government upon His shoulder, He must appear and receive the Church unto Himself. *These two events — His appearing and His return to reign on earth — make up the Second Coming of Jesus.*

When you hear ministers talking about the Second Coming, listen closely. Most of the time, they are actually referring to His appearing to catch up His Church, and not to His return to earth. I hear little teaching or preaching about the actual return of Christ to reign on earth. Most ministers today are looking for the appearing of Jesus; so they talk about the Second Coming in relation to His appearing. But these are two distinct events. Let's not misuse the terms and thereby confuse the Church.

There has been a great amount of confusion about this subject in the past, due to a lack of knowledge and understanding of God's Word. However, we are now in a blessed time when the Holy Spirit is opening our understanding to some exciting truths.

I believe you will be able to see the distinction between the appearing of the Lord Jesus Christ to catch away the Church and His return to the earth with the Church as we study these two events in the Word. A fixed period of seven years separate the two events. Both must take place because they have been prophesied, not only by sincere men of God, but also by the Lord Jesus Himself.

Let us consider His appearing. In the sequence of events, it takes place first.

9

Jesus' Appearing
Before the Tribulation

The Book of Revelation makes it clear that at the appearing of the Lord Jesus Christ, the Church will be caught up unto Him and will not be on earth during the seven years of Tribulation.

In the words of Jesus, and in the writings of Paul, we as members of the true Church are admonished to watch and pray, to look for His appearing, and to keep ourselves in a state of readiness. God's Word clearly defines His glorious appearing, so there need not be any further confusion concerning it. There are many references in the Scriptures regarding this sudden and glorious appearing of the Lord Jesus Christ. These Scriptures admonish us to be ready, vigilant, sober, watching, and praying. Christ's appearing *is* going to happen, and what an exciting event it will be!

The prime responsibility of the Holy Spirit today is to get the Church ready so that at the moment of His appearing, as the Apostle Paul wrote in Ephesians 5:27, the Church will be without spot, wrinkle, or blemish.[1]

For the Church to be ready for this moment will require a great amount of *ministry* by apostles, prophets, evangelists, pastors, and teachers. In Ephesians 4, the Apostle Paul states that the Church is perfected, not through tribulation and trial, but through the God-given, Holy Spirit-anointed *ministry* of apostles, prophets, evangelists, pastors, and teachers.

But this perfection of the Church will only come if we are willing to receive that ministry. If one is not willing, then he may expect much buffeting and difficulties from our adversary, the devil — all because of a lack of knowledge of God's Word. We must take advantage of the ministry God has provided for us. I urge you to get into a study of God's Word and receive the proven ministry of those who labor among you, those who come highly recommended by reputable men of God.

Some people reason that the Rapture will not happen. After all, they say, we are human, and as humans we could not survive a trip through the stratosphere without oxygen. Any person who says this is totally unaware of New Testament teachings concerning the glorious transformation that takes place when the Lord appears to receive His own unto Himself.

Others say that if the Rapture does occur it will not take place until the close of the Great Tribulation. Those who teach this are saying that we will rise to meet Jesus in the air, then come right back with Him. They have a limited knowledge of God's Word, particularly of the Book of Revelation. Revelation makes it clear that there are many activities in which the Church must participate in heaven, such as the Wedding of the Lamb, followed by the Marriage Supper. According to Revelation 19, both events take place in heaven during the Tribulation Period. Since we have to participate in those heavenly events, we will have to be taken there. It cannot be done by long distance!

Zechariah and Revelation make it clear that when Christ returns to earth to receive the governments of the world unto Himself and begin His earthly reign, those who have been in heaven will return with Him (see Zech. 14:5; Rev. 17:14; 19:14).

Revelation also reveals that the man who has become the Antichrist not only blasphemes God and His tabernacle, but **them that dwell in heaven** (Rev. 13:5,6). How did "them that dwell in heaven" get there without a rapture — or catching up — of the Church? Teachers may reason that these are the spirits and souls of the dead in Christ. We would be naive to use one passage of Scripture as a cover for our lack of understanding. Let's go to the whole of God's Word.

If you search for a single verse of Scripture which states specifically that the appearing of the Lord Jesus Christ and the catching up of the Church is prior to the Tribulation, your search will be in vain. There is no such verse. But by studying the whole of God's Word (which you should do), you will discover that the appearing of the Lord Jesus Christ is a certainty. The taking up of the Church to meet Him in the air is for sure, and it very definitely comes before the Tribulation Period can begin.

You will want to go back and read this again and again until these marvelous truths thrill you. You will then be able to share the truth with many other believers who are distressed and filled with despair. Not knowing if the Lord is coming and, if He is, whether it will be prior to the Tribulation, they are concerned and confused.

Many people lack an understanding on this subject, wondering if the "poor Church" will have to "suffer through the trials of the Great Tribulation."

Know the Truth

Some of the most negative teachings you can imagine have been presented on the "Tribulation suffering of the Church."

I proclaim that the Church is in the driver's seat. *From now until the appearing of Jesus, the Church of Jesus Christ is to become the strongest and most outstanding influence upon the face of the earth!* Check it out in God's Word and see for yourself. Realize that the prayers Jesus prayed[2] are going to come to pass and the statements He made concerning the Church (as declared in Matthew 16:18 when He said He would build His Church and the gates of hell would not prevail against it) are going to be fulfilled. You and I are already beginning to experience these things.

I want you to be absolutely convinced that He is going to appear. Unless you have that fact firmly fixed in your mind, there is little reason for you to be concerned about the Second Coming.

We find in the teachings of the Apostle Paul that he is very emphatic about our being informed so that day should not take us unaware (see 1 Thess. 5:1-11). The Word of God is our source of information about this appearing, not dreams, visions, or revelations, but God's Word. When there are dreams, visions, and revelations, they must be judged by the Word and found to be in harmony with the Word. If they are not, we do not give them any consideration.

---

[1]Spots, blemishes, and such are clearly defined and described in 2 Peter 2:9-19.

[2]Examine the prayer of Jesus recorded in John 17. You can be sure God will answer that prayer.

10

A Cause for Excitement

In John 14:1-3, Jesus said:

Let not your heart be troubled: ye believe in God, believe also in me.

In my Father's house are many mansions: if it were not so, I would have told you.

I go to prepare a place for you. And if I go and prepare a place for you, I will come again, and *receive you unto myself;* that where I am, there ye may be also.

This is a thrilling passage of Scripture, especially in this time when people everywhere are distressed. Jesus said, **Let not your heart be troubled.** He said, "Believe in Me, even as you have believed in God." This is God's cure for a troubled heart. Jesus was speaking to Jews who had trusted in God but were having difficulty accepting Him.

He also spoke this to His followers, but they did not have full spiritual understanding of Him or His teachings.

The answer to the many perplexing problems and the great stress and strain of today is Jesus — nothing else — not money, social status, psychiatry, New Age, or even religion. People today are trying all kinds of religion, but the answer is not there. The answer is in Jesus Christ, the Son of God, who came and shed His blood so that you and I might have life and have it more abundantly (see John 10:10). These truths edify and thrill my soul and spirit!

Jesus said in John 14:2,3, **I go to prepare a place for you. And if I go and prepare a place for you, I will come again, and** *receive you unto myself;* **that where I am,** *there*

57

ye may be also. This is an important verse of Scripture. Jesus told the disciples that He was going to prepare a place for them, and that when He did, He would come back and receive them unto Himself.

He did go away, and we have the record of His ascension in Acts 1:9. Since that much of the prophetic statement is already fulfilled, we have every reason to believe the rest will come to pass. We know He went away and we know He sits at the right hand of the Father, interceding for us and serving as our High Priest (see Rom. 8:34; Heb. 4:14). We also know He said, "I will come again."

What is He going to do on the occasion of His appearing? He said, "I will receive you unto myself." His words do not indicate that He is going to come here and abide with us. The key word is *receive*, which, in the Greek, means "to take" or "to receive beside."

His words do not at all imply that He will come and abide here with us or that we are going to be given some special place of hiding during the Tribulation. Many teachers confuse the Church with the remnant of Revelation, chapter 12. The thought that the Church is to be hidden away is an absolute misapplication of God's Word. By carefully studying the Book of Revelation, you will find that it is the remnant of Israel — not the Church — which is placed in hiding for three and one-half years.

We understand that we are to be received beside Him. This agrees with Jesus' other teachings on this subject. In Revelation 3:21, He said, **To him that overcometh will I grant** *to sit with me in my throne,* **even as I also overcame, and am set down with my Father in his throne.** Since we are to sit in His throne in heaven, He will have to receive us to Himself.

Jesus concludes His statement about receiving us unto Himself: **that where I am** (not *where you are,* but *where I am*), **there ye may be also.** We know where He is and we are looking forward to being with Him in that very place. In this passage of Scripture, Jesus makes it clear that He is coming back to receive us — His followers, the Church — unto Himself, so that where He is, *there* we may be also.

He spoke these things when the Church had not yet been established. He was in the process of laying the foundation of the Church and He was to become the chief cornerstone. He was telling the disciples that, after the process had been completed and the Church had reached its glorious position, He would come and receive it unto Himself.

If there were nothing else in God's Word about His appearing and the events that are to take place at that time, this one passage would be enough to establish these truths. Yet there is more.

Lift Up Your Heads

And when these things begin to come to pass, then *look up,* **and** *lift up your heads;* **for your redemption draweth nigh.**

Luke 21:28

At His appearing, Jesus will not come down to earth. He will appear in the immediate heavens and catch the Church up unto Himself. The Holy Spirit and angels will play a major role in this event. Angels were involved in both Elijah's translation and the taking up of Jesus, and they will also be involved when the Church is caught up. **And while they looked steadfastly toward heaven as he went up, behold, two men stood by them in white apparel; which also said, Ye men of Galilee, why stand ye gazing up into heaven? this same Jesus, which is taken up from you into heaven, shall so come in like manner as ye have seen him go into heaven** (Acts 1:10,11).

The disciples were not able to understand this and they inquired of Jesus, **saying, Master, but when shall these**

things be? and what sign will there be when these things shall come to pass? (Luke 21:7).

In order to answer their questions, Jesus took upon Himself the office of a prophet. This was necessary because their questions dealt with future events. The prophetic answers, given by Jesus, covered a vast frame of time which included the Church Age and our generation.

Allow me to point out that Matthew 24, Mark 13, and Luke 21 are "sister" chapters. These chapters are often referred to as the "Olivet Discourse," and came about as a result of the questions asked by the disciples.

In Luke 21:28, Jesus points out the proper attitude of a believing follower. **And when these things** *begin to come to pass,* **then** *look up,* **and** *lift up your heads;* **for your redemption draweth nigh.**

The signs Jesus gave which would BEGIN to come to pass were:

1. Jerusalem no longer controlled by Gentiles.

2. Fear becomes a killer, causing heart failure.

3. Men [through the space program] creating signs in the heavens.

4. Nations distressed and perplexed due to the upheaval of masses (sea) of people.

These prophecies did not come to pass in the days of the disciples, but surely we are seeing them fulfilled in this generation.

Jesus prophesied to His disciples as though these events could come to pass in their life span. Why did He prophecy in this manner?

Because He did not know when the signs would begin to occur which would create the season for His glorious appearing to catch away His glorious Church (see Mark 13:32,33; John 14:3; Eph. 5:27).

It was not until after the disciples received the infilling of the Holy Spirit that they were able to understand Jesus' teachings of the spiritual kingdom, His appearing, and His eventual return to earth to establish His earthly kingdom. This shows how vitally important the infilling of the Holy Spirit is to our understanding of God's Word.

So Jesus speaks to us today. He says, "Be excited but not alarmed. When these things begin to come to pass, look up and know that your redemption is at hand." This does not mean to walk around with your head turned toward the sky, but to maintain a proper attitude, a spiritual awareness of what is about to happen.

Jesus said we will see things beginning to come to pass. The emphasis is on the "beginning," not on the end, when all has been fulfilled. If Jesus did not appear to receive the Church until the end of the Tribulation, all things pertaining to that period would have been fulfilled. Our study of Luke 21 teaches us to look for His appearing when prophecies *begin* to be fulfilled — not at the end of the Tribulation, but before it. When we see these things *beginning* to come to pass, we are to look up, for our redemption draws nigh. The final act of redemption is the glorification of the physical body. (See 1 John 3:2; Heb. 9:28; Luke 21:28.)

Bible prophecies are rapidly being fulfilled. Everything happening in our world is pointing to the appearing of our Lord and Savior Jesus Christ.

We need to obey the Word and begin to look for His appearing, lifting up our heads from the despair, confusion, negativism, and defeat which has ensnared so many in the church for years.

It's time to recognize that our redemption — the final work of the salvation purchased for us at Calvary — is about to be completed. At His appearing, we will be caught up and our bodies will experience the final application of salvation: when mortality puts on immortality and corruption puts on incorruption (see 1 Cor. 15:51-53).

We are told that when we see things beginning to come to pass (such as the re-establishment of the nation of Israel, particularly the retaking of the city of Jerusalem; the space program now probing the heavens; and the many problems that have brought such distress to the governments of the world), we are to look up and lift up our heads, for our redemption draws nigh.

The Bible teaches that the generation which experiences the restoration of Israel will also experience the appearing of Jesus. I believe His appearing is coming in our lifetime.

Watch and Pray

In Luke 21:36, Jesus says, **Watch ye therefore, and pray always, that ye may be accounted worthy to escape all things that shall come to pass, and to stand before the Son of Man.** It is important to understand this verse of Scripture. Jesus said to watch. That means we should not be slumbering or sleeping, or in other words, taking things lightly. Neither are we to become weighted down with the heaviness of teachings that, instead of edifying, place us in despair, fear, and negativism. We are to watch and pray, so that we may be **accounted worthy to escape all these things that shall come to pass.** The key word here is *escape*.

I have heard people say that escapism is not for them, that they will trust God. That is a strange statement to make, considering the word *escape* is actually used by Jesus. It is even found in the original language from which the Scriptures are translated. Paul also uses "escape" in Hebrews 2:3. To neglect one's salvation is to cut off one's way of escape.

Jesus said, "Watch and pray that you might be accounted worthy." Do we consider ourselves worthy? If not, what can we do to make ourselves worthy? Our own righteousness will never avail, but His will. We need to realize that we are righteous because He is righteous. Paul tells us in 2 Corinthians 5:20,21: **We pray you in Christ's stead, be ye reconciled to God. For he** (God) **hath made him** (Christ) **to be sin for us, who knew no sin; that** *we might be made the righteousness of God in him.*

Our righteousness, holiness, and sanctification are based in Him. Jesus makes it very clear that watching and praying will contribute to our being worthy. Remember, God keeps the books and He is evaluating our spiritual lives. We are judged by Him, not by our peers.

As we carefully observe Bible prophecy being fulfilled and the workings of the Holy Spirit being performed, we will become excited and blessed! When we pray, we enter into communion with our heavenly Father. Prayer conversations can be two-way, if we allow it.

What a blessing it is to find ourselves in a relationship with God the Father, God the Son, and God the Holy Ghost. Watching and praying are two important things God's children are to do.

Because of the wonderful relationship we have with God, we can recognize that we are worthy. It really is not complicated, but is a simple matter of doing what Jesus instructs: "Watch and pray." When we do what we are told, we will be rewarded. The reward is to escape all the things that shall come to pass — not to just "endure" or "make it through," but to *escape.* The word *escape* does not imply "to be protected in," but rather "to quickly go out from." *We are not going to be protected during the Tribulation; we are going to escape it!* Read carefully 1 Thessalonians 5:1-11. The Rapture is *an escape from God's wrath!*

I am sorry for those who do not believe in the catching up of the Church. They have to disbelieve or explain away more Scriptures than they use to support such an erroneous belief. In some instances, verses are taken out of the original setting, changing how they relate to the rest of the Scriptures. To do this only causes confusion. Sound teaching always edifies, blesses, and is harmonious with all other Scriptures.

The word *escape* implies a quick action. God's Word teaches us from many passages that so shall His appearing be:

In the twinkling of an eye (1 Cor. 15:52). **Immediately I was in the spirit: and, behold, a throne was set in heaven** (Rev. 4:2). **As a thief in the night** (1 Thess. 5:2).

We are admonished to be ready on a daily basis. It is not something we do today that lasts from now on. We simply keep ourselves in a state of daily readiness, watching for His glorious appearing, so that we may be caught up to meet Him in the air and stand in His holy presence at the throne of God.

By the way, soul-winning will keep you ready and wise.

11
Jesus' Appearing
at the
Sound of the Trump

Another passage of Scripture which tells of our Lord's appearing is 1 Corinthians 15:51. The Apostle Paul writes: **Behold, I shew you a mystery; We shall not all sleep** (die), **but we shall all be changed.**

Paul shows that believers who are asleep (the dead in Christ) will be resurrected, which points out the doctrine of resurrection. Also, the statement establishes that there will be many believers living at the time of the event; and both the resurrected and living saints will be changed, pointing out the moment of physical glorification.

Many recognize that Paul was expecting the imminent return of Jesus during his lifetime, since he exhorted the Church to be ready and remain ready for the Rapture. (See 1 Cor. 15:52; Heb. 2:1-3; 9:28; 12:22-24; Phil. 3:20.) Besides this revelation, he also knew of Jesus' teachings (John 14:3; Luke 21:36; Matt. 25:10; Luke 12:35-40) and that no one could know the day and hour of His appearing (see Matt. 24:36). He knew God was a God of order and would not send Jesus for the Church until that event came up in the prophetic process.

As an Old Testament scholar, Paul knew that before Jesus could receive the Church, Israel would have to be restored. The Holy Spirit revealed, the Church itself would have to be mature, united, and glorious before the catching up. Since the Holy Spirit could have possibly brought about these events in his lifetime, Paul exhorted the Church to prepare for Jesus' appearing. He also knew that if these events did not occur during his lifetime, they would occur in the time of other believers.

We are those other believers, because prophecies pertaining to the restoration of Israel are being fulfilled in our time.

Paul continues in 2 Corinthians 15:52, **In a moment,** *in the twinkling of an eye,* **at the last trump.** The Rapture is a quick action, a sudden event, not drawn out; it will come as a thief in the night. (1 Thess. 5:1-11.)

For the trumpet (the last trump) **shall sound, and the dead shall be raised incorruptible, and we shall be changed** (v. 52). Paul, by the Holy Spirit, reveals the dead in Christ being raised incorruptible and the living saints being changed. Paul was still alive at this time, so he was including himself with those who were living in Christ, not the dead in Christ.

The Last Trump

This verse is often used by those who teach that the Church will not be caught up until the end of the Tribulation. They say the last trump is the seventh trumpet of the Book of Revelation, chapter 11. Such teaching is erroneous. The seventh angelic trumpet in Revelation is not the same trumpet described by the Apostle Paul here and in 1 Thessalonians 4:16,17.

Verse 16 says, **For the Lord himself shall descend from heaven with a shout, with the voice of the archangel, and with the trump of God: and the dead in Christ shall rise first.** This is exactly what Paul said in 1 Corinthians 15:52, that the dead shall be raised incorruptible.

Now look at verse 17: **Then we which** *are alive and remain* **shall be caught up together with them in the clouds, to meet the Lord in the air.**

It is amazing, but true, that the descriptions of the events surrounding the sounding of Paul's trumpet are one and the same (see 1 Cor. 15:52,53 and 1 Thess. 4:16,17). How very beautiful and exciting! At the sounding of that trumpet, the dead in Christ will be resurrected and the living saints will be changed and caught up to meet Jesus in the air.

Some say, ''But it's the *last* trumpet.'' Yes. However, Paul further elaborates in 1 Thessalonians 4:16 that this is the trumpet of God, not an angelic trumpet. These two must not be confused. All seven trumpets in the Book of Revelation are *angelic* trumpets which release some part of God's wrath or bring about events involving the Tribulation Period. (The Church will not have any part in the Tribulation Period, as a study of the whole of God's Word bears out.)

In 1 Corinthians 15 and 1 Thessalonians 4, Paul is talking about the trumpet of God. Trumpet calls are mentioned a number of times in the Scriptures. In these references, God uses His trumpet as part of the welcome for the conquering and overcoming Church. What a glorious event that will be! The dead in Christ will be raised and the living saints will be caught up together with them in the clouds to meet the Lord in the air.

First Thessalonians 4:18 says, **Wherefore comfort one another with these words.** The word *comfort* could be interpreted ''exhort one another.'' The appearing of the Lord Jesus Christ, the resurrection of the dead in Christ, the catching up of the living saints, and all of us rising in the clouds to meet Him in the air is an exhilarating truth that strengthens and excites us. When someone teaches that it is not going to be that way — that the Word really does not say that — it fills us with despair and leaves us feeling dejected.

Many saints who listen to teachings contrary to the Word seem so burdened. They have no joy and little or no evangelistic vision. They wonder, "When will we have to go into the Tribulation Period? It's going to be so bad!"

Someone else will say, "Oh, it's not going to be so bad, because we know our God is going to keep us through it all."

How long is it going to take the Church of Jesus Christ to realize the thrilling truth that God is keeping us every day? We do not have to go into the Tribulation to find out about the power God has to keep us. Let Him do it now and enjoy it! Look forward to the time when Christ will appear and catch us up to meet Him in the air.

We have seen that the trump of God, as described in 1 Corinthians 15 and 1 Thessalonians 4, is not the same trumpet as described by John in Revelation 11. The seventh trumpet in Revelation 11 is blown by an angel to signal the finale of God's wrath. It does not have the same significance or serve the same purpose as the one described by the Apostle Paul.

The seventh angelic trumpet signals the end of the Tribulation Period, the beginning of the Battle of Armageddon, and the return of Jesus to earth. The Books of Zechariah and Revelation declare that the saints are returning to earth with Him. If they had not been in heaven with Him, how could they return?

When people ask about Matthew 24 and 2 Thessalonians 2, I tell them to relate these passages to the whole of the Bible. They say, "but that changes the meaning." Whose meaning? Certainly not God's. Never take a passage of Scripture out of context. Remember, the Bible interprets itself, if given the opportunity. However, one must study the Word to discover its truths.

12
Watch Therefore

First Corinthians 15:52 describes the *last* trumpet. Let me emphasize that the description of the events at the sounding of this trumpet is not the same as the description of the events at the sounding of the seventh angelic trumpet in Revelation 11. This is the *trumpet of God*. It will be sounded by God, not an angel. It has nothing to do with the Tribulation, but has everything to do with the Church.

In 1 Thessalonians 4:17 the key phrase is *caught up*. In the Greek, it simply means "to snatch away." Though some do not believe in the "Great Snatch," that is what this Scripture teaches. I believe in the "Great Snatch" because that is exactly what the Apostle Paul is teaching.

If nothing were going to happen, Jesus would not have pointed out that we ought to be sober and vigilant, watching, praying, and working in the harvest fields. Something is going to happen to those who are really involved and committed. I am delighted to know exactly what the Word of God has to say. There is no way to refute it without changing the Word — there *will* be a catching up.

The Ten Virgins

Another passage of Scripture which supports the appearing of the Lord Jesus Christ is Matthew 25:1-13, the parable of the ten virgins:

> **Then shall the kingdom of heaven be likened unto ten virgins, which took their lamps, and went forth**

to meet the bridegroom. And five of them were wise, and five were foolish.

They that were foolish took their lamps, and took no oil with them: but the wise took oil in their vessels with their lamps.

While the bridegroom tarried, they all slumbered and slept.

And at midnight there was a cry made, Behold, the bridegroom cometh; go ye out to meet him.

Then all those virgins arose, and trimmed their lamps. And the foolish said unto the wise, Give us of your oil; for our lamps are gone out. But the wise answered, saying, Not so; lest there be not enough for us and you: but go ye rather to them that sell, and buy for yourselves.

And while they went to buy, the bridegroom came; and *they that were ready went in with him* to the marriage: and the door was shut.

Afterward came also the other virgins, saying, Lord, Lord, open to us. But he answered and said, Verily I say unto you, I know you not.

Watch therefore, for ye know neither the day nor the hour wherein the Son of man cometh.

The wise virgins were ready. Matthew 25:10 says that while the foolish virgins went to make their purchase, the Bridegroom came. Those who were ready (the wise virgins) went in with Him to the marriage and the door was shut. The key phrase is *they went in with Him* to the marriage. The Bridegroom did not come where they were; they were escorted by Him.

In John 14:3 the Lord said He would come again to receive us unto Himself so that where He is, *there* we may be also. First Corinthians 15 and 1 Thessalonians 4 tie in with John 14:3 because there is going to be a meeting in the air, and we are going to be where He is.

The Bridegroom did not come to the place where the virgins were to give them special keeping or help in their time of trouble. They (who were ready) went in with Him to the marriage.

According to Revelation 19, the marriage ceremony of the Lamb is a heavenly event, not an earthly one. It must take place in heaven before the throne of God. We will be caught up to participate in heavenly events before God's throne. This further convinces me that there is going to be an appearing of Jesus and that we will be caught up and escorted by Him to heaven.

I exhort you in earnest: don't play games with God and don't play "church." Get involved with what the Holy Spirit is doing today. Allow Him to work in your life on a daily basis and keep you ready for the appearing of Jesus. Don't fall into the category of those who would be called *foolish* because they were not ready. This does not mean they were not a part of the Church (there is every indication that they were) or that they were lost; it means they missed the Rapture.

I am not teaching a split Rapture, but I believe it is possible for a child of God to miss the Rapture if he becomes foolish about his relationship with the Lord. Foolish Christians will not be lost, but they certainly will not meet the Lord in the air. Those who are left will endure part of the Tribulation and will have to take advantage of the other vehicle for leaving this earth which, according to Revelation, is provided during the Tribulation. Study Revelation 7:9-17 and you will see how very clear this truth is.

In 1 Thessalonians 5:9,10, the Apostle Paul gives further insight into the appearing of the Lord Jesus Christ and the fact that we will not participate in anything on earth after that event. It says:

> **For God hath not appointed us to wrath, but to obtain salvation by our Lord Jesus Christ, who died**

71

for us, that, whether we wake or sleep, we should live together with him.

This agrees with what Paul writes in 1 Thessalonians 4 and 1 Corinthians 15:51,52. Whether we are the dead in Christ or living saints, we shall live together with Him. We are not appointed to wrath but to full salvation. The final act of salvation is the appearing of the Lord Jesus Christ, when we are caught up to meet Him in the air. Then we return with Him to appear before God's throne in heaven.

The key words in 1 Thessalonians 5:9 are *"not appointed."* Paul was instructing the Church that we are not appointed to wrath but to obtain salvation by our Lord Jesus Christ. There are those who teach that the Church will be here during the Tribulation and that God will provide perfect keeping for it. I understand this reasoning, but because it is not Scripturally sound, I cannot accept it.

Watch — Pray — Escape

Look again at Luke 21:36: **Watch ye therefore, and pray always, that ye may be accounted worthy to escape all these things that shall come to pass, and to stand before the Son of man.**

Watch is a word of action involving commitment, alertness, and readiness, while *prayer* is "communication with God." Proper communication releases great power. These two assignments, properly carried out, equate to *worthiness.* Jesus said, **Those who are worthy will escape all that *shall* come to pass.**

If you are a committed person of prayer, accept the benefits of your obedience. You *are* worthy — worthy to *escape* all things that shall come to pass (that's future) and be received by Jesus to stand with Him in heaven at God's throne (see John 14:3).

Notice Jesus said *escape all.* We who are worthy are to escape *all* — not part, but all — of the things of the future, once the Church Age is concluded. If we were not to be caught up until the end of the Tribulation to escape that which follows, we would escape the 1,000-year reign as kings and priests (see Rev. 2:26,27; 5:10). So we escape the trials, troubles, and tribulations which are coming on the earth.

Also look at the experience of John, recorded in Revelation 4:1,2. Notice John's description of his experience. It parallels the event of 1 Thessalonians 4:16,17 (which takes place before God reveals what is to come), with Luke 21:36, and the two are in perfect harmony.

When one carefully studies the Book of Revelation, a discovery is made: the Tribulation Period cannot begin until the first seal of Revelation 6:1,2 is opened by Jesus. When this event occurs at God's throne, the Church is standing there observing it.

Let's look at another passage of Scripture on the appearing of Jesus. In Revelation 3, the Lord Jesus Christ is giving a message, through John, to the church at Philadelphia. He did not rebuke the Philadelphian Christians or call to their attention anything that displeased Him. They were getting the job done. They had an open door, an outreach, an anointing. The important thing about the Philadelphians was that they kept the Word of God.

In verse 10, the Lord says, **Because thou hast kept the word of my patience, I also will** *keep thee from the hour of temptation,* **which shall come upon all the world, to try them that dwell upon the earth.**

There are several key words I want you to notice in this verse. First is the word *from.* The meaning of the Greek word used here is "out from."

Another key word is *hour.* This is not the Greek word for "sixty minutes," but for "a period of time." The Greek word for sixty minutes indicates a glance, a fleeting moment, but the Greek word used here clearly indicates a longer period of time. Since Jesus is not referring to a literal hour, we understand that He is speaking about "the temptation that shall come upon the whole world to try them" — that is, the Tribulation. The Church is to be "kept out from" that "period of temptation."

A third key word is *temptation*. The Greek word actually means "trial" or "proof." The Church will not need proving because it will already have been proven.

In Ephesians 4:11, we find that God has set in the Church apostles, prophets, evangelists, pastors, and teachers for its perfection or spiritual growth. In Ephesians 5, we read how Jesus will present unto Himself a glorious Church without spot, wrinkle, or blemish. The Church being glorious at the time Jesus presents it to Himself indicates clearly that the ministry of apostles, prophets, evangelists, pastors, and teachers has been accepted. Therefore, the Church will be mature, united, and even increasing.

The Church will not need to be proven and tried by the Tribulation. It is being proven and tried now, and all of God's Word bears this out. *The Church is going to be "kept out from" that period of trial because there is no need for the Church to experience it.*

13

Jesus' Appearing
Foretold in Prophecy

The next Scripture concerning the appearing of Jesus actually covers two full chapters of Revelation. The 24 elders are the most important group described in these two chapters.

Chapters 4 and 5 refer to the 24 elders who sit around God's throne. The number 24 immediately tells us they are representatives. The number 24 is the double of 12: 12 representing the Old Testament saints and 12 representing the New Testament saints. The word *elder* in the Bible always identifies "one who has been set in the company of God's children for their leadership and exhortation." We know there will be more than 24 saints in heaven — there will be a vast company of God's children. So these 24 elders are literal representatives of that vast company.

John sees this company already around God's throne before the Tribulation Period begins. If these 24 are representatives, then where are those they represent? We saw in Part I that John described them as "the great crystal sea." He refers to this sea several times in Revelation. In one place, he says this crystal sea is mingled with fire; and we know the Holy Spirit (fire) is responsible for all the saints who will be there.

The description of these elders confirms what is already taught. They are said to have crowns of gold, wear white robes, sit on thrones, and are associated with the prayers of the saints. They sing a new song of redemption, which the angels cannot sing. In that song they are clearly identified as being from all nations and peoples. They are from the earth, declaring that they have been redeemed by the blood of the Lamb and that they are kings and priests who are going to reign with Christ on earth. The redeemed saints of God have been victorious through Jesus Christ over everything that Satan has produced or tried to do.

What a description! John sees them, not on earth, but before the throne! They are there before the first seal of Revelation 6 is opened to begin the Tribulation Period. As you can see, the Church must arrive in heaven or there will never be a "Tribulation Period" on earth.

God's Dealings With Israel

Daniel 9:24-27 establishes the period of time before and during the Tribulation. Daniel clearly defines the Tribulation as a distinct seven-year period of time beginning with the Antichrist, the son of perdition. This man of sin comes on the scene and enters into an agreement with Israel. It is clearly stated that he does this at the beginning of the week. Daniel 9 reveals the 70 weeks of God's "determined dealings" with Israel. This is a prophecy which must be fulfilled. Many people do not believe that what is happening in the present nation of Israel is a fulfillment of God's Word, but I want you to know that it is.

Many Christians are ignorant concerning the importance of the nation of Israel. They are unaware that God has anything else to accomplish on the part of Israel. The subject is avoided by contending that Christians are the Israel of today and that there is no other. However, a study of Romans 11 proves otherwise. In his writing, Paul warns Christians not to confuse themselves with the natural seed of Abraham. The Church can be identified as the spiritual seed of Abraham, but there is also a natural Israel with which God has not yet finished His determined plans. He must finish His work or His Word will fail.

We are literally watching God beginning the restoration of Israel, setting the stage to complete His final seven years of determined work and thus fulfill the prophecies of the Book of Daniel. Since all the previous 69 weeks of Daniel's prophecies were seven years each, we know the last week will last seven years also. We are not allowed to shorten or lengthen the span of time set in Daniel 9:24-27.

In this same reference, we find that the man of sin,[1] who becomes the Antichrist at the beginning of that seven-year period, enters into an agreement with the nation of Israel.

Where will the Church be at that time? We have determined that the Lord will have already appeared to receive the Church unto Himself.

The Church — the Restraining Factor

Daniel 9 is important, for it establishes exactly when the man of sin begins his activity. This man of sin who is to enter into an agreement with Israel cannot do so as long as the Church is here. Second Thessalonians 2:1-9 makes it clear that the Antichrist, the man of sin, cannot be revealed until that which hinders or withholds him is gone. The man of sin is part of the spirit of iniquity which was evident in Paul's day. That spirit of iniquity is lawlessness. We have no restraint for lawlessness on the earth today, except for the Holy Spirit-empowered Church.

There once was a time when lawlessness could be controlled by reminding a man of his moral responsibility. As recently as the 1930s and '40s, a man's word was his bond. Then as moral law and responsibility broke down, we turned to judicial law. We depended on legal documents and procedures to protect us. Now, even judicial law and order are oftentimes circumvented.

The only true restraining factor for sin, godlessness, and lawlessness is the work of the Holy Spirit through the Church. Isaiah 59:19 says, **When the enemy shall come in like a flood, the Spirit of the Lord shall lift up a standard against him.**

It is the specific assignment of the Holy Spirit to develop and work through the Church. Once He finishes that assignment (and He *will* finish it), His earthly assignment will then be to concentrate on the seven years of dealing with Israel.

The Word tells us that when the Holy Spirit has the Church at the peak of its maturity, it will be glorious enough to be received by Jesus. When the Holy Spirit-empowered Church is taken out of the way, the man of sin (the Antichrist) will be revealed. The removal of the Church will inaugurate the Tribulation Period for those who are left behind.

Comparing Daniel 9:24-27 with 2 Thessalonians 2:1-9 establishes the fact that the Antichrist cannot begin his operation as long as the Church is on earth. Since Daniel reveals the Antichrist at the beginning of that seven-year period, we must conclude that the Church has been taken out of the way into heaven.

In 1 Thessalonians, chapter 4, we read Paul's description of the appearing of Jesus and our being caught up to meet Him in the air. In 2 Thessalonians, chapter 2, he admonished the Thessalonian church to stand fast and not be shaken by those who were teaching that the ''day of the Lord'' had already come. He reminded them that this could not happen until ''first there come a falling away'' and ''the man of sin'' be revealed.

In verse 8, Paul tells us that the Spirit of the Lord's mouth — His Word — and the brightness of His coming shall destroy the man of sin:

> **Even him, whose coming is after the working of Satan with all power and signs and lying wonders, and with all deceiveableness of unrighteousness in them that perish; because they received not the love of the truth, that they might be saved.**
>
> **Verses 9,10**

Two Separate Events

In these verses, Paul writes about two different events involving the Lord Jesus Christ: in verse 1, His appearing and our being gathered together unto Him; and in verse 8, His return to earth, at which time He destroys the Antichrist.

Paul was getting the saints in Thessalonica straightened out because certain people had come with erroneous teachings and had been confused. The same thing is going on today. Some sincere men are teaching erroneous things, traditions that are biblically unsound.

With just a little help from the Holy Spirit, it is not hard to understand this passage of Scripture. Both events — Christ's appearing to rapture His Church and His later return to establish His kingdom — are written about by the Apostle Paul. The two are separate and must not be confused. Paul makes it clear that the man of sin cannot be revealed and released to begin his reign of terror (the Tribulation) until the Church has been raptured by the Lord. Then, after the seven years of Tribulation, Christ will return to earth to establish His earthly kingdom. The first act of that reign will be to destroy the Antichrist, the man of sin who opposed God and set himself up as God in the temple of Jerusalem.

Methods, vehicles, and nations to be used by the Antichrist are being prepared right now, but the man of sin is not yet revealed. He is still being withheld and will be withheld as long as we (the Church) are here and the Holy Spirit is at work in the Church. But once we have been taken up to meet the Lord in the air, the man of sin will be revealed (see 2 Thess. 2:7-8).

We saw in Revelation 6 that when the Lord Jesus Christ opens the first seal, He is standing before God's throne. He is not sitting on the throne but standing before it with His company, as described in Revelation 4 and 5. He has left the throne in heaven to descend and receive His company, the Church, unto Himself. He returns and then walks to the throne, takes a book from His Father's hand, and makes ready to open the first seal.

The first seal produces a great deceiver, a man riding a white horse, using a bow but having no arrows. He is sent forth conquering and to conquer. He has no crown, so one is given to him. That certainly could not be Jesus. Jesus has many crowns. And He never uses a bow, only a two-edged sword. He does not go forth to conquer, because He has already overcome and conquered everything (John 16:33; Matt. 28:18).

The man who begins his activity at this time is none other than the Antichrist. His release heralds the beginning of the seven-year Tribulation Period on earth.

---

[1]The man of sin, or the Antichrist, is Satan's man. The "he" of verse 27 is really Satan. Satan can do nothing of himself, so he must have someone to carry out his evil plan; in this case, it is the Antichrist.

14
Jesus' Return

We have looked at the appearing of Jesus, which is the first of two events that make up His Second Coming. The second of these is His return to earth. It is altogether different from His appearing.

> **So Christ was once offered to bear the sins of many; and unto them that look for him shall he appear the second time without sin unto salvation.**
>
> **Hebrews 9:28**

Here we learn two things — we are to look for His appearing and, at His appearing, He will have absolutely nothing to do with sin. When He came the first time, He had to become sin so that we who believe might be set free from sin. He became sin so that He might pay the total price for those who would believe in Him. He was the great substitutionary sacrifice offered once and for all for our sins.

At His appearing, He will perform the final act of salvation, which is the glorification of our bodies. Today our spirits and souls are enjoying full salvation but our bodies are not. Full salvation for our bodies means they become glorified and immortal.

When Jesus returns to earth, He must handle sin, not the way He handled it the first time, but by destroying the followers of Satan, those who are destroying the earth.

The Battle of Armageddon

Now let's read from the writings of Zechariah, an Old Testament prophet:

Behold, the day of the Lord cometh (the day He returns to establish His Kingdom), **and thy spoil shall be divided in the midst of thee. For I will gather all nations against Jerusalem to battle** (the Battle of Armageddon); **and the city shall be taken, and the houses rifled, and the women ravished; and half of the city shall go forth into captivity, and the residue of the people shall not be cut off from the city.**

Then shall the Lord go forth, and fight against those nations, as when he fought in the day of battle. (You can see that the Lord gets involved in the Battle of Armageddon.)

And his feet shall stand in that day upon the mount of Olives, which is before Jerusalem on the east, and the mount of Olives shall cleave in the midst thereof toward the east and toward the west, and there shall be a very great valley; and half of the mountain shall remove toward the north, and half of it toward the south.

And ye shall flee to the valley of the mountains; for the valley of the mountains shall reach unto Azal: yea, ye shall flee, like as ye fled from before the earthquake in the days of Uzziah king of Judah: and the Lord my God shall come, and all the saints with thee.

Zechariah 14:1-5

The saints had to be in heaven with Jesus or they could not be returning to earth with Him. When the Lord returns from heaven to stand upon the Mount of Olives for the Battle of Armageddon, all the saints will return with Him. This is a thrilling and exciting revelation of truth. This event harmonizes with the seventh angelic trumpet of Revelation 11.

Changes in Light

In Zechariah 14:6 the Battle of Armageddon begins:

And it shall come to pass in that day, that the light shall not be clear, nor dark.

During a brief period of time, there will be no natural light from the sun, moon, or stars. According to Revelation 16:10, natural light will be withheld from "the seat of the beast," meaning the geographical area over which the Antichrist has gained control. Some think he will control the whole world, but he never does. He would like to, but God interferes.

The area of the world controlled by the Antichrist (the Middle East, the Mediterranean, and Europe, in particular) will be totally dark for a number of days. On this last day of Tribulation — the day Jesus is to return — there will be some light, but it will not increase. The sky will remain a sort of eerie gray.

But it shall be one day which shall be known to the Lord, not day, nor night: but it shall come to pass, that at evening time it shall be light.

Verse 7

Why would it be light at a time when it ordinarily would be getting dark? Because the Battle of Armageddon will be over by then. Those who have been destroying the earth will have been destroyed. The Antichrist and False Prophet will have been thrown into the lake of fire. Satan will have been bound and cast into prison for a thousand years. Jesus will have taken over the governments of the world and begun His thousand-year reign. It will be so glorious that at evening the sun will be bright!

And it shall be in that day, that living waters shall go out from Jerusalem; half of them toward the former sea, and half of them toward the hinder sea: in summer and in winter shall it be.

Verse 8

The great earthquake that divides the Mount of Olives will make a port out of the city of Jerusalem. Waters will flow from one sea to the other — the Mediterranean to the Dead Sea.

And the Lord shall be king over all the earth: in that day shall there be one Lord, and his name one.

All the land shall be turned as a plain from Geba to Rimmon south of Jerusalem: and it shall be lifted up, and inhabited in her place, from Benjamin's gate unto the place of the first gate, unto the corner gate, and from the tower of Hananeel unto the king's winepresses.

And men shall dwell in it, and there shall be no more utter destruction; but Jerusalem shall be safely inhabited.

And this shall be the plague wherewith the Lord will smite all the people that have fought against Jerusalem.

Verses 9-12

All of the armies[1] Satan could gather to come against Jerusalem for the Battle of Armageddon have been gathered in the valley of Megiddo, stretching into the plains of Jezreel. The Lord stands on the Mount of Olives. He speaks the Word and it goes forth out of His mouth like a two-edged sword to destroy the armies that have been gathered under the Antichrist for the Battle of Armageddon:

Their flesh shall consume away while they stand upon their feet, and their eyes shall consume away in their holes, and their tongues shall consume away in their mouth.

And it shall come to pass in that day, that a great tumult from the Lord shall be among them; and they shall lay hold every one on the hand of his neighbour, and his hand shall rise up against the hand of his neighbour. And Judah also shall fight at Jerusalem; and the wealth of all the heathen round about shall be gathered together, gold, and silver, and apparel, in great abundance.

And so shall be the plague of the horse, of the mule, of the camel, and of the ass, and of all the beasts that shall be in these tents, as this plague.

Verses 12-15

Jesus speaks the Word from the Mount of Olives which releases the plague to smite the vast armies of the Antichrist (Zech. 14:12). They are immediately blinded; their eyes consumed away in their sockets. They are immediately dumb; their tongues consumed away in their mouths. In fright, they reach out and grab one another for security. That only frightens them more, so they turn to fight among themselves. Their flesh begins to fall away from their bones. Their blood gushes to the earth, creating the pool of blood described in Revelation 14. It stretches over an area of about 185 miles in the valley of Megiddo and the plains of Jezreel.

In Zechariah 14, we have seen the events that take place at the Lord's return to earth. You can readily see the distinct difference between His return and His appearing.

Now let's look at Revelation, chapters 19 and 20. I want you to be well established in the authority of God's Word so that you will not be shaken by doctrines of error.

In Revelation 19:11, we pick up the final day of the Tribulation and the return of Christ to earth:

And I saw heaven opened, and behold a white horse; and he that sat upon him was called Faithful and True, and in righteousness he doth judge and make war.

We are able to identify the rider of this white horse. (The rider in chapter 6 could not be personally identified because that rider was the Antichrist.) This rider is called Faithful and True. He is our Lord Jesus Christ! What does He do? **In righteousness he doth judge and make war.**

A God of Wrath

Many people believe that our God has nothing to do with war. Others see Him only as a God of love. They think they can live the way they like and God will do nothing. Those people need to read the whole Book. There is more to the nature of God than just love. He is a God of anger, wrath, and furious indignation. He is a God Who will not acquit the wicked. He *is* love, and we are permitted to meet Him in His love rather than in His wrath. However, we need to discover the real love of God and all the aspects of His divine nature.

John goes on with his description in Revelation 19:12,13,15:

> **His eyes were as a flame of fire, and on his head were many crowns; and he had a name written, that no man knew, but he himself.**

> **And he was clothed with a vesture dipped in blood: and his name is called The Word of God.**

> **And out of his mouth goeth a sharp sword, that with it he should smite the nations: and he shall rule them with a rod of iron; and he treadeth the winepress of the fierceness and wrath of Almighty God.**

The closing verses of Revelation 19 are a preview of the Battle of Armageddon and the winepress that creates a pool of blood in the valley of Jezreel. Jesus is the one who treads the winepress. Standing on the Mount of Olives, He speaks the Word of God that releases the plague of Zechariah 14:12 to destroy the armies gathered for the Battle of Armageddon.

> **And he hath on his vesture and on his thigh a name written, KING OF KINGS, AND LORD OF LORDS.**

> **And I saw an angel standing in the sun; and he cried with a loud voice, saying to all the fowls that fly in the midst of heaven, Come and gather yourselves together unto the supper of the great God; that ye may**

eat the flesh of kings, and the flesh of captains, and the flesh of mighty men, and the flesh of horses, and of them that sit on them, and the flesh of all men, both free and bond, both small and great.

And I saw the beast, and the kings of the earth, and their armies, gathered together to make war against him that sat on the horse, and against his army.

And the beast was taken, and with him the false prophet that wrought miracles before him, with which he deceived them that had received the mark of the beast, and them that worshipped his image. These both were cast alive into a lake of fire burning with brimstone.

And the remnant were slain with the sword of him that sat upon the horse, which sword proceeded out of his mouth: and all the fowls were filled with their flesh.

Verses 16-21

Satan and Sin Defeated!

The opening verses of Revelation 20 read:

And I saw an angel come down from heaven, having the key of the bottomless pit and a great chain in his hand.

And he laid hold on the dragon, that old serpent, which is the Devil, and Satan, and bound him a thousand years,

And cast him into the bottomless pit, and shut him up, and set a seal upon him, that he should deceive the nations no more, till the thousand years should be fulfilled: and after that he must be loosed a little season.

And I saw thrones, and they sat upon them, and judgment was given unto them: and I saw the souls of them that were beheaded for the witness of Jesus, and for the word of God, and which had not

worshipped the beast, neither his image, neither had
received his mark upon their foreheads, or in their
hands; and they lived and reigned with Christ a
thousand years.

Verses 1-4

You can see what happens at the return of Jesus. Satan
is bound and cast into prison for a thousand years. All the
martyred saints of the Tribulation Period are resurrected and
enter into a relationship with the Lord Jesus Christ and all
the other saints. These events coincide with the return of
Christ to earth.

There are distinct differences between the appearing
of Christ and His return. The Church is caught up before
the first day of the Tribulation Period. Then Christ returns
to earth to reign on the last day of the Tribulation.

Look for Jesus! Be among those who are watching,
praying, and looking for His appearing. Join other Christians
in the harvest fields laboring and enjoying the work of the
Holy Spirit. Don't listen to erroneous teachings that strip
away that blessed hope which is yours — the glorious
appearing of our Lord and Savior Jesus Christ (see Titus
2:13).

---

[1]The Antichrist will bring ten armies to the Battle of Armageddon (see Rev.
17:10-14.) He will also have the support of the orientals of Revelation 9:13-19 and
16:12,16.

Summary

The Second Coming involves two major events: the appearing of Jesus to receive the glorious Church, and the actual return of Jesus to reign for 1,000 years on earth.

At His appearing, the mature and gloriously productive Church will be caught up to return with Jesus to heaven. This clears the way for the revealing of the Antichrist and the beginning of the Tribulation.

Christ returns to earth seven years later with all of His saints. At that time, He will destroy the armies of the Antichrist at Armageddon. He causes the Antichrist and the False Prophet to be cast alive into the lake of fire. Then, as Satan is bound and cast into the bottomless pit for 1,000 years, Jesus begins His reign of peace and righteousness, exercising authority over all the nations.

It is not difficult to understand the difference between these two events. Daniel points out in chapter 9 exactly when the Antichrist will begin his activity, which is at the beginning of the seven-year Tribulation Period. How wonderful is Paul's statement in 2 Thessalonians 2:7,8 that the Church must be removed before the wicked one can be revealed.

With the Church taken out of the way and the release of the Antichrist, both events occurring at the onset of the Tribulation, we can clearly see that the Church has absolutely no place on earth during the seven years of Tribulation.

The Church is not pictured on earth after chapter 5 of Revelation until it is described returning with Christ in chapter 19. God is not confused, neither does He make mistakes.

I pray that this book will help you to understand the Second Coming of Jesus, which includes His glorious appearing to rapture His Church and His return to reign on earth. I pray that you now understand that both are part of the Second Coming of our Lord, but are two different events separated by seven years.

My prayer is that you are not only looking for His appearing, but are also reaching out to others so they, too, may become aware of the appearing of Jesus Christ which is soon to take place.

Thank You, Heavenly Father, for Your beautiful and simple Word. Thank You also for the Holy Spirit Who provides us with proper understanding. To You, Father, be all glory and power!

Hilton Sutton is regarded by many people as the nation's foremost authority on Bible prophecy as related to current events and world affairs.

As an ordained minister of the Gospel, Dr. Sutton served as pastor for several years before entering his present prophetic assignment. Today he travels throughout the world, teaching and preaching God's Word. He takes the words of the most accurate news report ever — the Word of God — and relates it to the news today.

Having spent over thirty years researching and studying the book of Revelation, Hilton Sutton explains Bible prophecy and world affairs to the people in a way that is clear, concise and easy to understand. He presents his messages on a layman's level and shows the Bible to be the most accurate, up-to-date book ever written.

Hilton Sutton and his family make their home in Humble, Texas, where he serves as chairman of the board of Mission to America, a Christian organization dedicated to carrying the Gospel of Jesus Christ to the world.

To receive Hilton Sutton's
monthly publication, *Update,*
write:

Mission to America
Hilton Sutton Ministries
736 Wilson Road
Humble, Texas 77338

*Please include your prayer requests
and comments when you write.*

Other Books by Hilton Sutton

God's Master Performance
in *New King James Version*
(formerly *REVELATION — God's Grand Finale*)

ABC's of Bible Prophecy

Death of an Empire —
The Prophetic Destiny
of the Soviet Union

Familiar Spirits, Witchcraft and Satanism
Innocent Beginnings, Deadly Results

Pre-Tribulation Rapture of the Church

U.S. in Prophetic Events

Available from you local bookstore.

Harrison House
Tulsa, OK 74153

In Canada contact:

Word Alive
P. O. Box 670
Niverville, Manitoba
CANADA R0A 1E0